Train of Thoughts

This collection of work is dedicated to all the people that I have encountered so far on my journey of life that has sparked a creative thought or conversation adding to my ever-growing train of thoughts that have their own destinations.

Thank you for riding with me even if only for a few moments.

Vee
Veronica Thornton

Copyright © 2021 by Veronica Thornton

All rights reserved. No part of this book may be reproduced in any manner whatsoever without written permission except in the case of brief quotations embodied in critical articles and reviews.

First Printing, 2021

ISBN-13: 978-0-578-96242-9
Library of Congress Control Number: 2021915500

Train of Thoughts

∽

Veronica Thornton

Vee's Consulting

CONTENTS

Dedication	ii
Preface	xi
Prologue	xiii
Checking Coordinates	1
Somewhere	3
Reserved For Unicorns	4
Hidden Clues	5
A Bowl Of Soup	6
I Ponder	8
Under The Influence	9
Strings Attached	11
What Program	12
They Said	14
Numbers Game	15
No Time	17
L Ain't For Love	18
Gifted Rhythms	19

No Words	20
From The Ashes	21
Vibe Tuning	22
Missing Ones	23
A Mother's Tree	25
The Composer (Compose Her)	26
The Locksmith	28
The Stranger	29
Taste Test	31
His Kitty	33
Pied Piper	34
Hang In There	35
Action Words	36
Kisses	37
Awaiting The Return	39
No Errors	41
Engrained Stains	43
The Zone	44
Vision	45
Some Sense	46
Say Anything	47
Unbeaten Path	49
The Purpose	50

Disappearing Limbs	52
Telling Times	53
IT	67
Ridiculous	69
Ladies Night	70
Unconditional Love	72
Unfollow The Leader	73
Changing The Table	75
Diverse Opinions On Diversity	80
Suppose I Oppose	85
Vulnerable	88
Look	89
Unload	90
Fragile	92
Irreplaceable	94
The Contortionist	95
Serendipity	96
A Moment	97
Notes	99
About The Author	100
What They Said	101
Vee's Links	102

PREFACE

Train of Thoughts is a small collection of writings by Vee. Some of the writings included are previously published works that are among reader favorites along with some never released poems, essays and short stories. She collected a few thoughts on a variety of subjects in the very relatable rhythmic way she crafts words together in her unique style.

"I'm still writing my story why stop and spend my time explaining it to people that are only interested in judging the chapter they walked in on."

Vee

Prologue

Now Boarding...

My mind goes in a million different directions
I understand each way, but others think it needs correction
analyze each thought on its own
with all things combined another's mind would be blown
A train of thoughts arrives and leaves the station
no signs upfront stating a specific destination
riders without tickets hitching rides just for gratification
more often than not they intersect
arriving in places one would least suspect
there is no going just one way as the train will sometimes jumps the track
and various thoughts bring it back
the stops along the way are there for exploration
with messages that coincide with some form of explanation
 Those that have gotten on and off the ride
where the logical meet the illogical and sometimes collide
riders mixed with everything from the hypothetical
to the philosophical even thoughts that seem impossible
arriving to wherever they get off in my psychological having me think

along the philosophical
The thoughts keep coming so the train keeps running
as the station stays pumping
what's your thoughts a question, a statement
or a thought with an explanation
catching my train of thoughts
with many possible destinations.

Stating from the start some trains of thought
are not for the faint of heart.

Vee

Checking Coordinates

Many understand life doesn't go as planned
but forget the map was never in their hands
carefully navigating the way
the earth moves and the wind talks
missing souls that walk
every shift in decision
puts the map in a different position
steadily moving with no coordinates
many seem to miss the gravitational orbit
"X" marks the spot they say
then why did the route take you another way
turned right down the wrong road then
turned left right onto the highway
missing the signs that read
exit here the directions seemed clear
neglecting to account for the construction
taking place year after year
bridges burned; roads repaired
things built around things that soon won't be there
only specific routes through routes that will appear clear
But you had it all mapped out
every stop along every route.
Thought you knew where you were going in the beginning
checked off a few stops
that appeared to be steps towards winning
but when you weren't paying attention suddenly you take a turn

leading to a dead end
causing you to pause and recalculate your positioning
investigating just to find someone or something
has tampered with your navigational system
and now you are forced to start all over again
never considering your compass needed re-positioning
or maybe you were handed the wrong map in the beginning
you would think that's one of those things worth mentioning
but you were so focused on your own navigational system
Because as they say
"time's a wasting"
At times forgetting that navigating through life
is the only compass needed for an explanation
then suddenly one day you come to understand
the map you thought you had in your hands
may not have been mapped out just as you planned.

Somewhere

Constantly crawling, scratching, and clawing my way
trying to get somewhere
hoping when I arrive the air is clear
time move forwards even though what's behind is seems near
have to follow the shifts in the wind
it is blowing me away from where I began
trying to get through the maze with no clue of where it ends
following my heart or maybe I should follow the stars
they seem to always have some sense of direction
so it shouldn't be that hard
on some days I can stand straight
and walk in the right direction
but then there are other days when I hit a wall with no clue
whether as to if it is for my own protection
yet still I keep moving
hoping to get to a point where things go a lot smoother
even if I have to crawl, scratch, and claw my way there
I might get a little bruised up but it reminds me
I been somewhere and the only thing I can think in the end
is did I finally make it there
or is it just another stop along the way to
Somewhere.

Reserved for Unicorns

We don't all get that moment that we want to live repeatedly
time and time again
thinking about that one moment mentally
what's the usual number of unforgettable moments
we receive over a lifetime
I've yet to have any
so, I guess I'm slated to live a very long time
there is not one that I can think of
that I just want to reach out and grab
not one to replace the last unforgettable moment I never had
there are only a few that I cannot help but remember
but I would gladly replace them with memories that transcend
as they shine and glimmer constantly
wanting to replay a scene unhindered
holding onto an unforgettable memory
that will always be remembered
so how many moments like that do we get over a lifetime
I will tell you when I get mine until then
I have reserved a place for unicorns to live in my mind
as the unforgettable memory
that's yet to be mine will be one of a kind.

Hidden Clues

Sifting through the memories
to see if there was a memory of you that I refused see
memory lane does not look quite the same
looking through unattached eyes
the shadows covered what I could not see right in front of me
looking for truth where lies lie
going through each memory with a fine-toothed comb
wondering when what I once saw was transformed
within each memory a reality of how the present came to be
a wink and a smile, charisma that never went out of style
whispering words that made me stay around for a while
so much happening that the memories stuck together
and the clues were hidden unable to be seen
until the fog had cleared
and I was able to sift through the memories
only to find I was living a nightmare disguised as a dream.

A Bowl of Soup

It was more than just a bowl of soup
because it was filled with food for the soul
flavored just right
She said it was just a little of this and that
but I know it was more than that
a handful of strength with a sprinkle of wisdom
flavored with positivity that was given
a handful of warrior's dance
so the curves life threw didn't have a chance
spoonful after spoonful I ate
with every mouthful the ancestors
whispered this was not a mistake
after every swallow I felt the possibility of a better tomorrow
by time I finished the bowl
I knew I had misplaced sorrows
now filled with a bowl full of renewed energy
I was exhausted from being tired really
fell asleep rested well
woke up the next morning
and told those problems can go to hell
I felt a shift in my perspective
and recalled my original objective
at that moment I heard a few whispering words
"only the strong survive all the twist and turns ask the
elders for they have learned
this is not a privilege many have earned"

And to think I thought it was just a bowl of soup but there were souls speaking in every scoop.

I Ponder

My mind wanders when it wonders
wonders what if:
what it is
Is what it was
and do we see it that way just because
or does life just do what it does
When I wonder my mind wanders
and the thoughts seem to ponder
If it is what it is
and does what it does
what would it do if it never was
depending on who it's from
it may be disregarded
or someone will give an explanation that is half-hearted
because some are disheartened
I guess that's okay if they do what they say
and say what they are going to do
I wonder if they would still do it
if it didn't benefit them more than a time or two
I don't want my thoughts to put me asunder
so I wander while my mind wonders
and ponder on the thoughts I wonder.

Under the Influence

The supposed epitome of femininity
designed in the image of Barbie
nose symmetrical to her chin
every Barbie adorned forever with a gleaming grin
perfect posture pointed toes
shoes, accessories, and tons of clothes
made to look perfect wherever she goes
blonde hair, blue eyes, pale skin
the perfect accessory to Ken
distributed globally saying "Hey girls be like Barbie"
over time they added a few hues to the skin
of both Barbie and Ken
yet it doesn't change the message originally sent
the projected images we see are expectations
of only a fraction of society
while conditioning others to emulate accordingly
and reinforced socially
the perfect non-typical figure size zero to three
with the proper form considered to be the feminine norm
although not anatomically accurate
there is accuracy in the image they wish to project
expecting little girls to emulate
never suspecting the damage being done until it's too late
good ole Barbie the supposed epitome of femininity
creating victims of a distorted reality
while glorifying a self-hate mentality

yet the message seems to be this is what many aspire to copy to acquire a Ken, you must be like the image of Barbie or one of her friends.

Strings Attached

Fear a historical bully used to manipulate many
like puppets on a string
fear gets entangled in everything
misplaced hate causes the puppeteers to salivate
scared if the puppets cut their strings
in the other direction the pendulum will swing
when the puppets no longer live in fear
the love of humanity is all you will hear
as they cut the strings of the puppeteers.

What Program

Many were programmed to be deprogrammed
which wasn't part of their plan
so the deprogrammed have to deprogram the programed
and introduce them to a new plan
the plan to change the overall plan
to bring reality back from the misguided one's hands
there is no easy solution to the revolution
it must be done with sharpshooter execution
the orchestration of a demonstration
never was the move to change the nation
digesting what's been ingested was a valuable lesson
so many got the lesson and started professing
about the programming of the programs
being shoved down our throats by the media and TV land
don't you hear the drums pounding
shots getting louder yet they act like they could not be prouder
the man behind the curtain trying to see
what's left to be taken away disproportionately
across all minorities leaving a trail of homicide,
genocide claiming many to be suicides
but we know how they died even after they have lied
the tel-lie- vision does not affect my vision
nor does it change the overall mission
eye see what many don't see
the hypocrisy breaks down categorically
stemming from several European philosophies

that they stole religiously
while claiming it came to them mythically
in reality they rewrote history to exclude the origins
by saying how profound it was scientifically
the pendulum is swinging back the other way
sending them in a panic because
it's waking up the ones of today
that are coming to understand the games they play
they get shook when you read what is not in their books
hoping none give it a second look
big brother listening and wishing
the deprogrammed are not paying attention
to what their books and media fail to mention
to get the programmed listening
wake up to see the game they are playing
was originally created for those like me
so we study their ways and our history vigorously
but you don't have to take it from me
they say the revolution will not be televised
but eventually we will see.

They Said

I look like I have an attitude
I look like I could be rude
I look like I will dismiss you
I look like this look like that
they tell me what I look like regardless of how I act
they said that I must be angry that I don't fit in
I must be crazy walking around with an illuminated grin
stupid to think that I'd be accepted for myself
and not being like them or everyone else
I act like I can go around having a mind of my own
I act like I understand that my heart will always be home
I act like this weight on my back doesn't affect the fact
I act like that because I am proud of who I am
as well as proud to be black
I look like me mixed with cells from my ancestry
I look like I know a thing or two as my eyes see through you
I look like nothing I have been through
Maybe that is why what "they said" didn't bother me
while you repeat it apparently it irritates you.

Numbers Game

She was case #390493876 mother of 3. Their family still exists hanging by a thread. "Come to them for help" she remembered that's what they said but they threatened her existence instead "please take a number" is what the first sign read.

She took her number and sat in a seat where her thoughts started to wonder. How in the hell did she get taken so far under? The first thing in the morning and they were at number 93 while she sat there with the number 143. Wow, really, she takes a moment to breathe and checks to see if she has all the paperwork, she thinks she needs. Then she stops and cannot help but think about inmate number #243-125 he was just sentenced to 3-5 years of their lives just for helping their family survive

Suddenly she heard someone say #143 she jumped up and said yeah that's me. It was her turn to learn that the numbers game wasn't just a term. The lady behind the desk grinned quite devilishly and said how are you my dear? Now let me make a few things clear. I need your life history then there are a few hoops to jump through maybe 6 to 3, then I think because you appear resilient, we'll top it off with the pit of pestilence. As line 8 states that in so many years you become property of the state and in the meantime, we are going to monitor how you carry these 2 ton weights and we'll add 3 more tons if you choose not to participate.

She said wait. Maybe there has been some kind of mistake I'm #143. I came for the help you advertised and that's it really. I only needed a little assistance our family dynamic has changed through events that threaten our existence in this instance.

The lady said no. 143 was just your number in line I checked your ID and you are case number #390493876 it's been dormant but still exists. You had gotten yourself together according to this, but you seemed to thrive until the actions of inmate #243-125 who seemed to disrupt your way of life. Seemingly tail spinning into a hidden abyss. So here you are with me doing this. Tell me sweetie is there something that I missed?

Well since you passed the formalities for today. You can just call me #143 with whatever case number you have attached to me. I remember seeing a second sign that read "This is State Property" where I took the number under the overhead. For now, the intricacies of the situation are of no consequence since all you have are numbers as your evidence. Now back to business. I believe I filled out all the forms with the copies of requested documents that seem to be the norm. So, I guess the remainder of what you mentioned is just part of weathering the storm. As I stated I came for the assistance you advertised not for you to look at my numbers that you don't care to understand with judgmental eyes.

The lady smiled and said Well it looks like you have everything you need I'll make a few copies one for your file and the originals you keep. Then in 90 days when I do not get back to you just go ahead and call me. By then you should have downsized to the bare necessities and then I will give you just a fraction of the help your family needs. Well, that's if you're polite and your bank account doesn't have more zeros than my family's. I am only telling you the rules sweetie. If you want any more help, we can get you in deeper but it will cost you more when we give you useless tools. We must make sure your numbers never add above zero that is our number one rule. Now I've yet to decide what kind of hoops you will need to jump through. After all I am only here to offer a place in society that suits me but where they will attempt to keep you.

No Time

If I had time to waste
I would count the strands of hair as I pull them out my head
I would count each time I wished I was dead
I would count the number of times I lied and said I was fine
while pressing matters hid behind a smile many times
If I had time to waste
I would count each tear that fell
add them up year after year until they filled a thousand wells
I would count each time I bit my tongue
every time I was offended by someone
then multiply those times for every time
I put my foot in my mouth
divided by each time I just could not get the words out
I would count each time I stepped and fell
then calculate each time I was stepped over as well
I would even count each footprint that left tracks across my back
but I don't have time to waste
besides who has time for that.

L ain't for Love

If love is a chemical reaction
why can't I find it on the periodical table
searching through each element
each one has its place each one so pertinent
yet love seems irrelevant
so I wonder if its' something of which I'm even capable
they have symbols for everything down to the air we breathe
O represents Oxygen
it's so potent it can come out of the leaves of trees
yet we exhale CO_2 which is Carbon Dioxide
that the plants need to breathe an infinite cycle
floating around in the air
still there's no combination of chemical elements
for love they say is supposed to be floating around somewhere
an intangible yet attainable thing
as it has a physiological reaction so it seems
in reality it's a combination
of all chemical and elemental things
available to all living beings.

Gifted Rhythms

My heart beat to the ballad his love played
while the harmony caresses me slowly
time seems endless as the melodies change
each note carefully selected and played with perfection
the sounds resonate through my soul to the core
I get trembles from the bassline
listening again and again until I can see the treble dance
his song creates pictures in my mind
for my heart to resist it never stood a chance
I can see the purple in the skies
with rainbows running everywhere
the sun sets right over his eyes
so all I do is stare feeling like I'm right there
the clouds created his movie for me to see
as the rhythm of his song exudes from me internally
My heart beat to the ballad his loved played
while time never stood still
the sentiments always stayed the same
and the work he puts into my song is always on display.

No Words

Unable to take away the pain that seems so absurd
I felt helpless because all I have are words
a voice silenced a light now made dark
the birds no longer sing to a heavy heart
listening closely you may be able to hear
the whispering in the winds from passing years
you feel their comforting words as if they were right there
knowing their shadows will never again appear
a warm feeling in a cold place
while seeing their likeness within a child's face
the memories of loved ones could never be replaced
hugs, kisses, and calls on the phone
will not bring them back home
but reminds you that you are never alone
the thought of saying I'm sorry seems so absurd
even when combined with other loving verbs
wanting to offer comfort but all I have are words.

From the Ashes

Abused by life she always thought twice
it would be nice to follow her first mind
but the conversations between her mind and heart
made her reconsider decisions three or four times
questioning her first thought
sometimes she would cast a wide net
in hopes that the right decision is caught
at one point she was truly angry
the stones life threw broke her down over time
until she became a pile of rubble
on the ground creating dust from being kicked around
still angry that day she found herself being scooped up
moved to the side tucked away
but just enough to see the sun everyday
slowly but surely the anger mutated to something else
they say sitting there in a pile of inclement weather
she said there has to be a way to pull it all together
she took a breath that sounded like a sigh of relief
and meticulously reconstructed herself piece by piece
adding a few new pieces along the way
she sculpted her own sense of reliefs
she saw things start to take form
then piece by piece she was reborn
Restored, renewed, and reinvented
shedding the hurt from all those that once pretended.

Vibe Tuning

He kind of gave me that vibe
not that oh you seemed cool kind of vibe but
I'd be a fool kind of vibe
that naw something else is going on with you kind of vibe
that I wanna be nice but it ain't gone work kind of vibe
usually I listen to my vibe
because they have yet to be wrong kind of vibes
even when I don't know what's going on with my vibes
the one time I chose to go against my vibes
was because everything checked out ok because of lies
I questioned my vibes
and wondered why over time those vibes intensified
I asked myself was it wise to initially go against my vibes
because now their confused
he gives me good vibes in certain ways on certain days
but otherwise, it's an emotional haze
I had to take a moment to collect myself
fix my crown and change the hand life had dealt
all because I chose not to rely on my vibes.
I almost killed it so for a while it went running to hide
I had to nurture my vibe back to health
I knew it was better when a new hand was dealt
now I'm vibing with my vibes
giving them protection where they reside.

Missing Ones

Each memory means something different
to each person individually that others are unable to see
although we are a small part of a bigger whole
still there is no one who can fill the shoes of a mortal
turned immortal soul
The strength in a wise person is that they
are never truly alone unless they choose to be
so by design we are all connected wherever we go
regardless of who you claim you do or don't know
Love, joy, and laughter is what we're all after
but when our life is done the pain and grief come after
and to some their pain is the only thing that matters
The memories that are left to each
are never within another's reach
Those that left before
are waiting to greet some of the missed ones even more
and families become whole on another level
as they meet one by one under the sun
to make past and current bloodlines one
Each memory going down in history as it was meant to be
leaving the reality of a missing link in the family
as they transition to report to the ancestors what they missed
and tell them of memories of how much they've been missed
as they watch over whose left as we grieve over the newly missed
No one stands alone
families are made just for this

to remember our time is short in this life
as we grieve for those we deeply miss
because one by one
we will become part of the newly missed.

A Mother's Tree

I paid attention to the roots of our tree
the wisdom they dropped was planted in me as a seed
I wouldn't know what kind of mother I would be
if I hadn't had one to teach me
as I also watched her with her mother as they showed me
what a mother/daughter relationship could be
they taught me quite a few things
be careful of the company you keep
never wipe your feet where you sleep
always remember that unfiltered words cut deep.
There's a time and place to turn the other cheek
but when they are both under attack
never hesitate to unleash the beast
never forget to ask questions
pay attention to even the subtlest of lessons
some give answers while some leave things with questions
and be present in the present live with no regrets
let your children always see a Queen they respect
life is often unfair so
always expect to never know what to expect
and always remember Murphy's Law
even if the anything that can go wrong hasn't happened yet
follow the universal principles
and your roots will root for you
the mothers of mothers rooted from my tree
with the seeds, they planted living through me.

The Composer (Compose Her)

My equilibrium was off he had me walking left of center
how exactly I got like this I don't remember
my body seemed to be walking to his melody
he stroked every one of my senses as if they were piano keys
adding the sounds of rhythmic drumbeats
each bang of the drum energized things that were once numb
opening my eyes to what I was once blind, deaf, and dumb
his eyes transmitted energies
that seemed to vibrate all through me
every nerve felt as if it was on fire
the feeling was electrifying it was truly burning
with passion and desire
I remember tingling sensations flowing from his fingertips
along with the sway of his hands as he manipulated my hips
I transcribed the notes from his tongue strokes
but he used his pen for the lyrics we wrote
it felt like he spelled out every word
as I sang them out like his favorite songbird
creating the sound of a beautiful symphony
winning every category in every awards ceremony
that we hold more than occasionally
carefully crafted intimate music
he brings it out of me
resonating things internally I never want to get used to it
every time is never like the last time
so sometimes my equilibrium is out of line

causing me to walk left of center from time to time
but I love the thoughts left lingering after each time
as I play back the music repeatedly in my mind.

The Locksmith

He knew he had the right key
he slid it in the lock very gently
wiggled it around just a little bit
and said "Aww. The perfect fit"
She was biting her lips
allowing her back to slightly dip
in disbelief that his key fit
With the key in the lock
he rocked back and forth
while she allowed him to set a course
taking the movement of the key full force
once the lock was popped
the treasures came pouring out
as he exclaimed "that's what I'm talking about"
Running through her thoughts was
no other key ever seemed to pop her lock
now the search for her locksmith
could finally come to a stop.

The Stranger

It was all the same no matter the name
all their game sounded lame
But then one day he came
It struck me all of a sudden
One day while talking to my cousin
We were talking about who was real and who wasn't
Then he walked by with the most pleasant scent
A stranger not sharp dressed but he was decent
Oh, the places my mind went
Skin sun kissed, with sexy ass lips,
Long limbs from his fingers to his toe tips
Yes, I want him between my hips or better yet thighs
Either way I want to see him rise.
I want to look deep into his brown eyes
to see if he is sexually wise,
Nothing feels out of place while I feel him caressing my face
Memorizing his body at a slow pace
Without a care I'd kiss him everywhere
Making him very aware of things I would dare
While he gently pulls on my hair
My legs around his neck pulling him close
Telling him what he wants to hear the most
In my vision we have tried every position.
I was apprehensive about being so submissive
Oh, my goodness he was very inventive and attentive
Pleasing every one of my senses

eventually rendering me senseless
I swear it felt like Christmas.
Legs shaking, back aching, mind racing, soul quaking,
I swear this is love making.
No matter how we intertwine our bodies seem aligned
Fast and slow grinds in and out from front and behind
Always stopping time, I know I'm about to lose my mind
He must be one of a kind.
All these thoughts I contemplate
But we haven't even had a first date.
I sense there's no danger
while dreaming about this handsome stranger.

Taste Test

I just had to have a taste
I only asked for a piece
because I'm not one to waste
I started by stroking his head
so, he wouldn't be put off by what I said
then he looked at me and said
"Look here Dorothy
this ain't the yellow brick road
but you just stroke gold
you see the pictures I paint cause some to faint"
I had to tell him I'm all of what they ain't
See my tongue made the scarecrow lose his brain
the tin man's heart ran away
because my mouth swallowed it whole one day
and the lion wasn't a coward
until him and my kitty got to play
as his manhood was devoured
so, I hope you can grip what I'm about to release
I asked for a piece which was a tasty treat
I can't give you the kitty because you need a beast
Since this is not Oz and I know there's no wizard
the wholesome act kind of makes some quiver
you better drive it home, so I get the point
let me know when you're ready to blow this joint
He said "Baby I'm an O.G.
and I can handle you like Mario Andretti"

I told him well switch gears already
I want to see the pistons move up and down
rev my engine make it make that sound
so, I can watch the oil drip all on the ground
since I'm not one to waste
let me lick some off
then spread the rest like lotion on my face
He said "Damn baby you're aggressive,
you move kind of swift"
I told him it's your fault you're the one with the gift
you should have seen the look on his face
as he said
"Darling your pen can't be replaced you asked for a piece
but turned around and gave me a taste
I have to admit now I want a whole plate."

His Kitty

Whenever he sits near me
I must cross my legs to silence Ms. Kitty
he makes her purr so loud
I hear her purring even when he's not around
but I can't pet her like he does I've found
see Ms. Kitty has always been particular
about whom she allows to shape her perpendicular
but the way he strokes her so lovingly seems to fit perfectly
like two rhythms in perfect harmony
yes, he worked his charm on her and me
He said I'm all his favorite chocolate dishes
and he loved the taste of my Hershey's kisses
he licked and slightly bit each one
then talked to Ms. Kitty for a while before he started the fun
he played Ms. Kitty like a violin
each stroke fingered with such precision
changing the purr into a symphony
while each note resonated with me internally
as he looks in my eyes intently
and says I know Ms. Kitty likes me
then frame by frame like a choir I sang his name
while he knocked it out the frame
high and low notes came and went as we became one
the climax came and he proclaimed my name
So here we sit legs crossed with Ms. Kitty purring and shit
but only we know why I keep a smile on both sets of lips.

Pied Piper

The pied piper played his songs for me
we rehearsed them intimately
he stroked his instrument in an interesting way
making me a slave to the way the music played
doing whatever the tune would say
he wasn't just full of wind
as he caressed me with his melody again and again
every note danced across my skin
leaving my body tingling and internally singing
every commanding symphony of keys had its own harmony
that just seemed to resonate with me
I didn't want the song to be released
because of the feelings that it would unleash
intense pulsations of the beat
as I watched him stroke his instrument seductively
his mouthpiece was exquisite
it was designed to complement the breaths he blew into it
every breath I heard him blow
created sounds that would cause my feelings to grow
he fingered a rhythm like no one else
creating a chorus that climaxes by itself
I was a slave to the way the music played
doing whatever the tune would say
rehearsing them intimately
as the pied piper knows what songs to play for me.

Hang in There

I'll have to start at the end so I can recall how it began
all because I almost tapped out while he was tapping in
the rushing of waters sent my heart all a flutter
I tried to holler but
no words uttered just a constant stt stt stutter
legs clinched pointed toes feeling the pressure
a feeling always treasured a meter with no measure
in his eyes streamed electricity straight to my soul
burning his love in like water over hot coals
his aim is on point so transmission is his goal
I taste the sweet sweat dripping from his face
while he makes his home his favorite place
getting nicely nestled in
changing positions and rooms over and over again
he gently pulled my hair and said are you ready to go there
a servant to his love I whispered I love this right here
one by one buttons came undone
as he kissed my neck, he said two bodies can become one
touching me so gently my heart skips a beat so rhythmically
I asked why would you want to do that to me
smiling and giggling
he said he would make me tap out before he tapped in
Telling me this is how it starts, and you can see how it ends.

Action Words

He knew how to direct
as he slowly kissed her on her neck
the sound of a silent inhale and he knew it was on as well
she gave him a minute to change his mind
but he loved a challenge of her kind
it wasn't the curves in her behind
but the dimensions of her mind that are a rarity to find
so, he brought her in close
he started whispering and spitting that knowledge
suddenly her clothes were a ghost
she said I believe in fair exchange
you put something on my mind
now let me find a way to blow yours in kind
tell me what you want
I'll show you what I got
you tell me if I hit the right spot
the power of my verbs
got him screaming out continents with healing herbs
searching for a pot of gold in the land of no rainbows
but where creation may unfold
causing the lone volcano to explode
but he wasn't done he wanted some more
this wasn't the first time, but I wasn't keeping score
he said every time my lips formed words
they turned him on in all kinds of verbs
that's when I became his favorite nerd.

Kisses

I love when he licks my Hershey's kisses
the way his tongue feels it's so delicious
he makes my playground wet
before he gets to visit it and I just can't wait
for him to have fun in it
sometimes it's like a seesaw going up and down
making my head spin like I'm on a merry-go-round
I love hearing his pleasurable sounds
feelings roaring like a roller coaster
I never want the ride to be over
with no line I'd ride again and again
in the front as well as the end
the way he does my body is like a wet dream
and I taste him all the time it seems
voice distorted from my body being contorted
I can rewind the tape in my mind
and playback the tape any time
the way he feels is so divine
as long as I know he's all mine
sometimes I leave the words alone
and try to contain them in between moans
because I'd rather he read my mind
like he's analyzing my hormones
I love how he kisses my Hershey's kisses
it reminds me that all aren't so vicious
making me want to grant his wishes

not a genie in a bottle
but wishes coming true and going full throttle
and there are just too many to swallow
I guess he'll love me one of those tomorrows
until then it's my heart that I will follow
knowing his insides aren't hollow
I don't quite know what to expect
but I see no reason to run from it
because my emotions he seems to protect.

Awaiting the Return

I just got touched and the feeling is too much
he had me in his clutches
I couldn't help but squirm around
because he was just going to town
Now that his task was complete
I still seem somewhat incomplete
surrounded by my favorite things
they don't bring the pleasure he brings
I should call him back to finish the attack
starting with his fingers gliding down the small of my back.
delivering like the paper man
I'm liable to say whatever I can coherently understand
he's never quick on the trigger
which suits me just fine go figure
I can't help but lose control
it's almost like something has taken over my soul
and now this man is what is making me whole
without leaving the room
he takes me to a dimension beyond the realms of the moon
he shows no aversions to my sexual perversions
I can say yes sire your wish is my desire
and he makes it his goal to take us both higher
setting my insides completely on fire
sometimes he drives me so insane
that I can't even remember my own name.
I mean my mouth is dry, were inside but I think I see the sky

I don't even care why or how
I just know what's happening now
He must have read the blueprint to my body
because he knows exactly what to do when he is inside me
whenever he leaves it's like a feeling you won't believe
I can't get to my feet; my knees get weak
when I try to lie down, I can't help but squirm around
because for some reason
my body thinks that he is still around
I have to keep my knees together
because the thought of him may lead to self- pleasure
and it just doesn't measure to what I feel
when we are together
So, as I sit here with my favorite things
and think of the pleasure he brings
I guess I will continue to hold firm
and just squirm and yearn
awaiting the bedroom master's return.

No Errors

His fingers glide over my body like a keyboard
Typing seventy words a minute
on the test he got a high score

No Errors!

I told him what to type
and he adlibbed with the nibbles and bites
I love the stories he writes
As his fingers glide across and type away
I want his pen to come out and play
Oh, the words I want it to say
I want it to write all over me
while I read every word gleefully
A few to the right a few to the left
I want him to write until we both lose our breath
If I watch every stroke of his pen move up and down
the words spin around in my head
yet I can't make a sound

No Errors!

The story he tells is different every time
sometimes he types, other times its straight to the pen,
I love when he allows my liquid ink to step in
and lubricate his mouth

so the words from the pen just glide on in
the story is always a nail biter I love being his ghost writer

No Errors!

The paper moves from side to side
as his pen takes me on a magic ride
trying to get to the final destination
will the story end with a question or an explanation
sometimes mind-blowing frustration
leading up to the moment of my exclamation
I'm going in I can't take it
I have to suck the words from his pen
I must see how the story ends
and let the words seep from my mouth
as we come to the climax and then
oops the pen exploded again
ink all over the place
but I love how the words taste.

No Errors!

Engrained Stains

They laughed when they saw the blood on their hands
like kids playing with puppets on a string
dangling lives making them dance
they take whatever they can and eviscerate the lands
step back and say look at what you did
as we have done all that we could and all we can
yet the green keeps getting passed to the same kind
illustrious lives thinking with common thoughts
so no one minds
gifted with the luxury of obliviousness
postulating on golden pedestals
spewing facts no one will ever find
while claiming everyone else to be the fools
engrained in their brains
is to always stand on the backs of those they wish to maintain
blood stains run deep in their veins
never enduring the pain and labor they impose
so they only see a tolerable bloodstain left on their clothes.

The Zone

She waited for him to break down how she was to remain a friend
in the zone of no love lines where broken hearts go
as many unknown heavy costs
She had a skill for never letting them see her breakdown
no matter how many times she had been let down
she never showed them how her heart frowned
little did they know
she had gotten quite familiar with the ground
as it was the only thing that caressed her tears
while no one else was around
it also helped to keep her head out the clouds
just enough to never get fully knocked down
There is always a reason for it to be the wrong season
love life looking like a compilation of b-rolls
from someone's favorite comedy
although the main antagonist is seeking more than comic relief
covering up the overwhelming feeling of grief
but she has a smile that can make the biggest pessimist believe
she's unphased as it covers all her pain
until she can get away and release it all
allowing her tears to dance in the rain
while lost in the zone of friends where she remains.

Vision

Her eyes set sight on the destination that was just beyond a couple of sunsets. She turned her back on doubt and couldn't fathom regret as things got clearer for the moment she decided to move towards a destination she hadn't seen yet.

The journey had been a long one filled with a lifetime of education, feelings of isolation and people attempting to build her up with frustrations, yet she persevered with no thoughts of retaliation as she could only focus on getting to her destination which was just beyond a couple of sunsets. A place where there are welcoming arms waiting to embrace her for no reason. Something she often gives but rarely gets. Where unconditional love is a verb with no conditions on it and laughter is a part of conversations without having someone irritated by it.

Her vision was clear, so she kept moving towards a destination she didn't know, yet a place that she knew was just beyond a couple of sunsets. A place that would prove the journey was well worth it.

Some Sense

Her eyes and ears forever sealed closed
she had to be careful of where she put her nose
the words were said to sound so keen
but she could never see their faces
to understand what they really mean
she knew that to hear and to see
were two completely different things
to have one without the other
oh the confusion it brings
but then she thought
there are those with sight that still can't see
along with those that can hear
yet listen to nothing
she felt she must be blessed
to have neither of those things
but the senses she did have
allowed her to sense some wonderful other things.

Say Anything

Some people will try to tell you anything
they'll say the sky is green with pink lines in between
and how they saw a purple unicorn sing
about becoming an average human being
but I asked
what made the unicorn want to change its reality
there are clouds in a sky with no color what does that mean
isn't there a reason for everything
still they tell me I don't know what I see
stating I have to listen
as they explain how my mind plays tricks on me
yet their words don't add up as they divide their explanations
and proclaim "well that's enough" the rest is just technical stuff
while saying by the way
the rainbows chased all the dreams away
but I say you still haven't told me anything
can I see the purple unicorn sing
or does it just appear to some people
is it one of those types of things
why would the rainbows get mad and chase the dreams away
aren't dreams made that way
questions with no answers
while things are said and done faster and faster
telling you anything, messing with everything,
explaining nothing
isn't that something

when in reality the purple unicorn was singing
about finding it's dreams
while chasing the rainbow in the sky of mystical things
but was shot down by the green-eyed monster of human beings
and the trail of sadness it left behind
are the pink lines they tell you they were seeing
they'll tell you anything
if you never heard the song the purple unicorn tried to sing.

Unbeaten Path

Often I've been described
as a horse of another color
that just can't hide
even though sometimes that's not how I feel inside.
See many claim to love my originality
but the consensus is
they just don't know what to do with me
What's your brand, who's your market?
We just can't or don't cover all these targets
broken hearted starving artists
get smacked in the face the hardest
stolen tidbits repurposed and twisted
but as a proud horse does I walk away unoffended
and keep changing colors
because I'm too close to just starting to be finished
I just sometimes need to recenter
and get my soul replenished
but regardless of all that my drive is still not diminished
for a horse of another color the unbeaten path
has yet to be finished.

The Purpose

Why does a caterpillar turn into a butterfly
do you think it thinks it's about to die
or does it dream of flying through the sky
does the caterpillar have a rough life
before its wings sprout and take flight
it is low to the ground all furry trying to get around
it must be scared of getting stepped on but it has to press on
then it's forced into a cocoon
where there's not much room
for the metamorphosis that comes soon
not knowing what others will see it can't wait to break free
bursting out of the cocoon a new life it will assume
able to soar and fly free beautifully
do you think it ever has memories of all of its setbacks
other animal attacks or the times it barely got away
at times just surviving day to day
maybe that's why it flies that way
it glides through the air without a care
looking as light as a feather and beautifully put together
maybe the caterpillar's purpose
is to show us that life is worth it
it does mimic our existence exhibiting so much persistence
learning many lessons early in life
while learning to adjust to the struggles and strife
making changes under a metamorphosis
while in a cocoon fortress

then with new insight you claim your wings
spread them and take flight
beautiful and free
now understanding what life was meant to be
so why a caterpillar to a butterfly
starting out vulnerable and small
learning about life how to get around
knowing all the time its transformation bound
while gaining new insight then take off in flight
exploring new sights elevating to new heights
remember the goal is to soar and fly
being comfortable in your own skin, shining from within
seeing things from beginning to end
allowing the metamorphosis to set in
finding what you were meant to be
and embracing it beautifully
I think that's what the caterpillar wants us to see
at least that's a caterpillar's purpose to me.

Disappearing Limbs

Rooted as one tree yet limbs grow exponentially
one connected to the other
creating a beautiful arrangement of leaves of varying colors
together they support the environment and each other
sometimes sections of branches don't grow straight
or maybe their growth is stunted as they contort and bend
because the leaves were vulnerable after stormy winds
little invasive bugs came and left poison where they fed
even still there are those rare occasions
other branches of the tree try to prune their own leaves
the way they see fit never thinking what the roots think of it
causing chaos between the branches, the leaves, and the tree
choosing to be unaware that no matter what you cut off
the roots are still there and all they end up doing is
exposing the weaknesses of the tree
every branch, stem and leaf have a purpose
and they function as their part of the tree entails
because each branch supports the other
stemming from roots that look out for each other
just because you want some limbs to disappear
doesn't mean the roots didn't want them there
to have a view so slanted maybe
you never would have been planted.

Telling Times

They say people use to bury something called a time capsule. It was some sort of way to leave small parts of the history of a specific time for another generation to find. They probably had no clue of how people would evolve. Now we just make an appointment with a Memory Keeper if we want to experience things from past generations. There were all kinds of memory keepers. They had memory keepers that could recollect the emotions attached to things and who they belonged to, some who could trace a bloodline just from the touch of another person's sweat. I wonder if memory keepers will always be here or will there comes a time when they are phased out just like time capsules.

My grandmother is a memory keeper. It's said that she gained her abilities a few years after the laws changed. Apparently, that is when many people began to gain different abilities and the world started to become more peaceful and harmonious as it advanced. She showed us what seemed like movies of the way things have changed over time. Personally, it seemed impossible that the world could have been so cold and seemingly desolate although inhabited by people. She would show us times where people were killing each other over things we wouldn't even consider today. They would kill each other over everything from food and water to money and power. She showed us how every difference someone had offended someone else causing most of the fighting and killing. In school, World History was my favorite subject because of all the stories and movies my grandmother shared. As far as I know, I do not have the gifts of a memory keeper. But my Momma said, "I'm a late bloomer and all my abilities haven't been triggered yet". I couldn't help but wonder would any of us have our abilities if the laws had not changed when they did. My grandmother said it was always possible but the changes that came because of the laws that were put in place probably sped up the process. I'm inclined to agree with her as evolution will eventually happen and seeing some of what I saw of our history we needed to evolve.

"Tipoli Yemoja get your head out of your thoughts and help prepare for the celebration". Although somewhat startled that's what I heard from a distance. I almost forgot what day it was. Today is the 25th anniversary of the meeting of minds conference. The whole family was meeting up because it was the day my grandmother puts on a grand production in remembrance of the reasons for the celebrations in the making for our region. It was our yearly reminder of how we have been able to achieve our current state of heightened awareness and intelligence. Memory Keepers around the globe would put on a show for their regions. There were televised gatherings and parties of all sorts tuned into the same frequency of compassion. You could hear simultaneous outbursts for miles around shouting out the words that are etched into every educational institution across the globe today. "If we are putting a puzzle together, we need all the pieces to see the whole puzzle come together. If you do not use all the pieces of the puzzle, you will never see the true beauty in what can be created with what you already have". Those words were spoken by a woman only known by the name Kaya. She was one of the original spokespersons of a group once known as The D.P.A.M. Otherwise known as The Disappointed People of America Movement. My job during the celebrations was to help secure the region. One of the abilities that I possessed and could actually control was the ability to create and materialize any weapon from the past present or future that I could visualize. We had a Replicator as part of the security team as well. His name was Arish. His job was to replicate any weapons I need to produce and distribute them to the appropriate personnel as he also possessed the ability to teleport to locations in seconds. I must be on full alert over the next few days while the celebrations are going on across our region. I can't let my mind wander. There are people that wish to destroy the whole world just so they can fight over who controls rebuilding it in their image. Based on the combined teachings of the memory keepers around the world we already know that didn't work the first few times.

Arish and I just went around all the main areas to check that they were as secure as they needed to be. The stage was set. It was made of concrete to symbolize the strong foundation our nation now set upon. There were lights twinkling in the sky that just seemed to hover over the platform. There was a supersized screen that floated over the platform stage. That is where my grandmother will project her movie like memories of the day legislation was presented to the international news and governments to enact new laws that many said would "level the playing field". Our celebration is for the change that occurred because of "The Meeting of Minds" conference. "Tipoli, you must not worry everything will be as it should be," Arish said. I didn't find his words very comforting as I knew there were possible threats looming. They are the one common thread throughout the history of human beings that always causes problems.

I am being kind calling them people as they are really barbarians. They are constant disruptions of peace. They took their wealth with them to the land of Ill-Gotten Gains because they were furious, they no longer had the power their wealth previously afforded them once the laws changed. Now they are in an uproar because the world has flourished without them pulling the strings. I'm not sure if they are more upset, they are no longer in control or are they upset about most of them not being able to manifest special abilities. My grandmother told me years ago that it's a little of both. History has shown they have no regard for human life or attaining self-actualization.

At that moment I hear one of the security team members yell out

"It's time!" I glanced at Arish just as he grabbed my arm and teleported me to my position where I would be in direct line of sight of all the key points of security during the celebration. I watched as people started piling into the open-air arena. We all watched as the stars went from a twinkle to a sparkle. Every sound I heard seemed amplified. The crackling of the lights, accompanied by the clattering of bottles, keys, and things that seem to jingle. I could hear the chants of the people getting louder as the crowd grew larger. The ground began becoming covered with a rainbow of colors in both clothes and people. It was so beautiful. Amidst all the loudness there was a sense of peace as you can hear some congratulating others on their recent successes. Generations of families coming together all for this one event.

A member of our aerial security team named Matthew gave the "all clear". He and his brother had ex-ray abilities. They had scanned everyone coming into the arena for malicious thoughts. Most people didn't mind their thoughts being scanned for this event as it was a needed security measure. As far as we know there are only a few people that can read thoughts without disrupting the minds of others. Most of the people with those abilities were working with the government. They help keep our checks and balances checked and balanced. The celebration was starting. One by one every culture within the world performed various art forms from their ancestry. All leading up to the moment where we all get to look in amazement as my grandmother projects her historical memory of the day legislation was brought forth to forever change our civilization. A slow silence started to come over the crowd. My grandmother climbed the stage. When she got to the top of the stage she stopped and gazed at the crowd. Then she said "My grandmother Kaya was a wise woman because she understood the connectivity, we all share. She understood that to become as great as we are we had to build everyone up from where they were". That's when my grandmother signaled to all of us working security to be on high alert as she started to project onto the large floating screen her memories of that day as it was broadcast on all international news outlets.

"We have breaking news". Members of the D.P.A.M. are set to propose legislation that critics are calling groundbreaking."

We saw the bold letters scroll across the screen They are calling it the "Leveling the Playing Field Act". On the screen was a strong show of solidarity from all the representatives of the disappointed party standing alongside with those in government that were elected officials of various disappointed communities, cities, and states standing side by side with some who were part of the wealthiest percent that also supported the legislation. Everyone leered in awe of what they heard as the spokespersons for the D.P.A.M. made their opening statements. There was a tall, moderately built brown gentleman with a grey suit and a blue tie that read "Level It" in bold white letters. He was standing beside an older indigenous American woman dressed in her native tribal garments. There were two more men and women standing by the podium.

The brown gentleman in the grey suit stood tall and upright and before he started to open his mouth there began a slow, faint beating of a drum. Then just as he began to speak the older lady in the native tribal garments started speaking as if she was talking for the gentleman. It was like a human ventriloquist act. As he mouthed the words, she spoke the words with the faint sounds of a beating drum in the background. He stood at the podium, but she was in front of and speaking into the microphone. The first thing she said in front of the cameras and government was "What the Hell is wrong with America"? The room went silent except for the faint beating drum everyone now heard distinctly. People were looking around as if all were in awe of the words of this older woman dressed in her native garments as the tall man in the suit mouthed the same words as he also expressed them in sign language as she spoke. That's when her name went across the bottom of the screens of televisions around the world. In big bold letters as she spoke the words scrolled across

"Kaya" member of The Disappointed People of America Movement. After that moment of silence, she proceeded in speaking.

She said "If we are putting a puzzle together, we need all the pieces to see the whole picture. If you do not use all the pieces of the puzzle, you will never see the true beauty in what can be created with what you already have". This was followed by another moment of silence where the drum seemed to stop beating.

The tall brown man slowly and gently grabbed the woman by her hand and walked her to a chair sitting directly behind her. Then he slowly turned around, stepped to the podium, and raised the microphone to his height and began speaking. This time when he spoke it seemed as if his voice was a beating drum. With a deep voice, the tall brown man they called Louis said:

"What Kaya just said to you is what members of the D.P.A.M. had been pondering and discussing over the past several months. How can we utilize what we have in this great melting pot of a nation to be able to see the whole puzzle? What would we be able to create? What would putting together all the pieces of the puzzle look like? What are the stories we want to leave in this world as a representative of what America looked like and what it became? I know I don't want to be a part of the puzzle that doesn't get included in making the puzzle complete. But you know what we and the members of the D.P.A.M. in addition with those we represent have been those pieces of the largest puzzle that sometimes get lost by accident or the pieces that got tossed to the side because someone didn't think they were a part of the puzzle they were working on. The beauty of putting the puzzle together is seeing what you created when you finished. You know there are always those pieces of the puzzle that no one seems to know where they go but then suddenly. BAM!! You find out exactly where those pieces fit but some other pieces had to be put together first to see that. We at the D.P.A.M. have come to the understanding that although we all have differences in various aspects of life, we are all part of the same puzzle. And what that puzzle is my friends is making America the very melting pot it claims to be by giving everyone in it a level playing field. Why a level playing field you ask? Simply put we now know and understand that the game has been rigged the whole time. Within this puzzle we call America there are pieces of the puzzle that have been destroyed and damaged beyond repair for decades if not centuries. There are also some pieces to the puzzle that don't want the puzzle to reveal what else is there. So, as we deem ourselves a nation that prides itself on the idea that everyone pulls themselves up by the bootstraps and has the ability to achieve greatness. We figured why America doesn't just put their money where their mouth is! Let's create the equality we claim to have built this nation on to the ultimate test. We propose that we simply level the playing field from here on out".

Then the floating screen went dark followed by silence from the crowd. My grandmother turned around just as I could see the natural color return to her eyes. They tend to look like gold and black circles when she is projecting memories. Everything appeared to be okay. My grandmother began to address the audience stating that before "The Common Ground Amendment" was created America was on a slippery, downward spiral towards a dystopian society divided in every way possible. Divided by color, class, religion, sex, sexual orientation and so on and so on. If you were different from the next, then basically there was a category for you and you somehow you didn't fit into the "American Dream". It got so bad that everyone was fighting over everything even what they thought defined an "American". This led to the dumbing down of our society based on simple disagreements of ideas and who had control. During those times we were the laughingstock of the World. I think one day people woke up to the realization that all the people that were disenfranchised in our society were everyone that didn't fit the visual perception set forth of what the "American Dream" was and who could obtain it. This finally led to all the disenfranchised and disappointed to come together to find a solution that would benefit America instead of only benefitting some with the "Proud to be an American" attitude as it was previously defined. They knew that without change no one would be able to survive. My grandmother told the crowd in the arena. "We are that change that has changed the whole world." The crowd gave a resounding sound of approval evident by cheers and applause.

That's when the security team got an emergency message from one of the other regions that there had been some significant movement over in the land of Ill-Gotten Gains. Some say that's where all the well to do that didn't want anything to do with our new laws went to reside. They didn't want to give up a thing nor did they want to work for anything, but they wanted to control everything. I decided to send Matthew and Arish to check out the situation. I figured with Arish being able to teleport and replicate things combined with Matthew's ability to fly and scan for malicious thoughts it would be quick and efficient. The people of the land of Ill-Gotten Gains never gained special abilities so it was unlikely that aerial security would be detected. The trick was to spend as little time as possible there. Scientists had discovered some time ago that the longer a person stayed on the land of Ill-Gotten Gains the more their mind would become clouded with the hate that fills the air there. One would think that with all their wealth and shiny things they would be happy in their own world. I guess it's not a privilege when everyone around you is privileged.

Matthew and Arish were back within minutes. They reported they witnessed one of our former government officials talking to Leonard. Leonard was the oldest and wealthiest of the wealthiest. He had attempted to buy and overthrow our government because he didn't want his daughter to have to work for anything when she became an adult as the new laws stipulated and were made active years ago. He was the one that suggested him, and others start their own society which later became their prison as the rest of the world flourished without the use of the wealth of the land of Ill-Gotten Gains.

We had to immediately get the word out to all the regions. They had to keep their eyes open for anything out of the ordinary. The celebration of "The Meeting of Minds" is always a little hectic as people are gathering all over the world and being reminded of how far we have advanced as a society. I had to get my grandmother to safety and seek counsel before making our next move.

Rumor had it that Leonard was trying to revert our government back to a time before the "Common Ground Amendment" was enacted. The amendment gave people a fair shot at achieving what many deemed then as the American Dream which later became the World Vision. Based loosely on Maslow's Theory of Hierarchy people would reach a level of consciousness never before seen if everyone was provided with the same economic foundation. The D.P.A.M. had found a way to do that by providing every American with their basic needs. In short, the new laws insured every American citizen had what are considered to be basic needs: food, shelter, water, medical access, and a quality education that is reflective of our nation including our role in the world. Our educational system needed to be as multi-faceted as the citizens that resided in our nation Everyone was given access to free quality education that is inclusive of education from all cultures that are a part of this melting pot of a society. Every American is provided with free housing and healthcare with all that entails. The new western medicine became reflective of all the cultures meaning there was a combining of vast medical knowledge from various cultures that had been proven effective which in some cases eliminated illnesses and diseases that were thought to be incurable by solely using what was previous versions of western medical practices. Everyone was provided with the same monthly stipend of $3,000 for every person over 18 for ten years with no restrictions on how that stipend is spent. Those over 18 that came from wealth had to temporarily relinquish claim to their family wealth and their family would have to provide the housing and monthly stipend for 5 years. After that time they would receive the remaining 5 years from our government. Their family name would not give them any privilege as they had to start on the same level as everyone else and find their own way to be successful. Those were the main sticking points that seemed to matter to almost everyone when it came to the laws. Leonard and his cohorts were in strong opposition to the changes. They did not think it would be profitable, it was also the fact that over time it was revealed that members of these wealthy family names were not as driven, or they didn't know how to obtain success without their family name and wealth attached to it. As a result, many were not allowed to take over the wealth of their kin because as the law stipulated one had to create their own accomplishments first to do so.

I told Arish, Matthew, and a few others to escort my grandmother along with some of the elders to the "E" safe house for now. We need a meeting to discuss what this means. Arish and Matthew left to round up everyone while the rest of the security team ensured a quick and peaceful exit for everyone else that was in the arena. We did not want to alert anyone to the news we had received until we had more knowledge. Once I saw that the grounds were clear and there was nothing left but green grass for miles with bushels of newly planted flowers and plants, I was able to get to the safe house with everyone else.

The elders were all sitting in the gathering room. They were drinking what looked like cups of tea and discussing what they were informed of by Matthew and Arish. I did not understand how they could seem so peaceful given the information they had all just received. My grandmother called out to me. "Tipoli come and have a seat with us." As I sat down, she handed me a cup that was sitting on the table as if was made especially for me. My grandmother began explaining to us that Leonard was a very unhappily wealthy man. She began to explain that after the laws changed the look of government started to change. Average working people began running and winning elections. As a result, the government began looking like the melting pot it represented. The wealthiest of the wealthy were pushed out. After a while, they could no longer buy power or prestige because people started to change their outlooks on life. Once everyone's basic needs were met the mentality of everyone changed. They no longer wished to envy someone else's way of life. They wanted to create their own lives. Gardens and fruit trees became the norm everywhere. Technology advanced astronomically. Science was able to explain what was previously unexplainable which meant people were eating better, living better, and creating a world around them that would benefit everyone. When we started seeing all this happen the world took notice and followed. People were creating a world where money was not as needed as it once was for things to sustain life. This made people appreciative of what they had and the people around them. Everything was no longer a competition. It became how can we help each other, and all come out on top. That is when it seemed like only a few people here and there started to gain special abilities. Others just started to live longer and healthier lives.

There were questions and theories about why some people were gaining special abilities and why others were not. After years of research and studies across the globe, Scientist discovered that the people that were willing to take advantage of and were appreciative of their basic needs being met were the same ones that reached a psychological awakening causing their brain power to increase astronomically. These people were able to reach a form of self-actualization. In many ways confirming Maslow's theory of hierarchy. In some cases having the basic needs of people met allowed them to make every effort to reach their full potential and purpose. Scientists also discovered coded cells in the DNA of people that naturally have a malicious intent that only seek power and greed that was not present in those with special abilities. Once these discoveries were made public it was then that those that were not doing as well as others because of their lack of knowledge or ability started to create disruptions within our society. Those that had not gained any abilities were the people that had no idea of how or the drive to do anything for themselves. All they knew how to do well was take from someone else and claim it as theirs. They either wanted things given to them or they wanted to use ill-gotten gains to advance never allowing themselves to see their true potential. In essence, they had no desire to reach self-actualization on their own or to make valuable contributions to society. These people wanted control over the outcome of our world simply to feel privileged to something. If they couldn't do that, they were willing to destroy the world from within. Their only mission is to control it regardless of what they are left in control of. I guess in some way they felt they would be treated as Gods of some sort if they were responsible for rebuilding the very thing they destroyed. And Leonard wants to be one of those gods.

I could not help but ask my grandmother what were we supposed to do with people like that? Their thinking is dangerous. I cannot imagine things going back to the way it appears in your memories. My grandmother smiled and said, "Tipoli Yemoja as the pendulum swings one way it must eventually swing the other way". She said since the very founding of this country things have gone only one way and that one way was only good for one group of people until "The Meeting of Minds" happened. This country although young was indeed old by that time. As we just celebrated the 25th anniversary of the Meeting of Minds we will have equal time if not more as the pendulum has just started its journey back the other way. That is when all the other elders chimed in with nods and words of agreement. Somewhat irritated I shouted out "But is Leonard not a threat"? One of the elders tapped my grandmother on the hand and quietly said: "History only repeats itself if no one has learned from it and it seems the whole world has learned from it with the exception of a few". She said, "Ask yourself why do you think these people want to take away the very things that we all need to live, or why would they want to see other people suffer unnecessarily especially if it doesn't directly affect them"? She said let Leonard make his plans with the wealthiest of the wealthiest people of their lands. Let them make their attempts to disrupt our society. That is when you will see the eyes of people that are fulfilled meet the eyes of those that are never fulfilled. For every set of eyes pointed at us, there are ten thousand to one pointed back at them. We will be telling them as many we stand as one against the few that want the power to control things that should not be controlled by malicious ones. Then maybe you will see what we do with people like that. I knew that they all had very valid points as I shook my head in agreement.

I was still left thinking I could easily send someone to grab him and have his brain scanned by a member of our security personnel. Something tells me that my grandmother and the elders would not approve of doing such a thing. They are ultimately saying just let it play out. I know we have what we need now but I cannot see living without food or having to beg for it. I do not understand why we have to pay for education and then get only a limited view of the world. Not to mention all that homelessness. We would not even have a word for that now if it wasn't part of our history. I do not know what to do right now besides sit her think and sip on what I think is tea.

That's when I thought to myself: "Maybe I should make one of those time capsules I used to read about. I do not know if we'll always have memory keepers as it is evident that things change over time. What if they somehow lose their abilities or die without the gift being passed on. If not worse and Leonard somehow reverses time, and no one gains the gift of realizing their purpose? Yes, I think I will create a time capsule and bury it in the open field where my grandmother gave her speech for the 25th anniversary of the ideals that made everything possible for me to be here today". Then suddenly a wave of emotions and visions of things I never saw before flashed right in front of me in what seemed like seconds. Everyone in the room seemed to be unbothered and was smiling at me as I was sitting in amazement. My grandmother looked over at me and said: "You have just been given the gift of seeing the future".

Suddenly I hear "Tipoli Yemoja get your head out of your thoughts and help prepare for the celebration". That is what I heard from a distance. I almost forgot what day it was. Today is the 25th anniversary of the meeting of minds conference.

IT

So many said she had IT and when she was ready, she would know what to do with IT. Many described IT as this light that seemed to twinkle effortlessly from her eyes. She figured they were just trying to find some nice things to say because everything else sounded so lame to say. All she could think is what is this IT that I have and why don't I see IT. They speak of this IT as if everyone doesn't have IT. But what is IT?

She was just being herself and expressing her thoughts as they pertained to the world. She didn't look particularly special as she saw herself but even when she's not thinking about IT. IT seems to always be around. Everyone has been talking about IT and how they saw IT but no one will say what IT is. So she went to find IT because IT was everywhere and not going away. No matter what she could not seem to find IT. There was no question that IT was there but she didn't know how to find IT or even where to start looking for IT.

IT appeared to be this unimaginable thing that she is just supposed to know when she finds IT. But why can everyone else see IT so clearly and not her? She tried so many things to find out what IT was. Each thing she tried she dug her heels in went full throttle and gave IT her best. She began to find part of the problem was there were many things she was good at yet none of them seemed to be IT. The search for IT became something she was chasing. No matter how fast she tried to get to IT nothing appeared to be IT. She would get so far and then hit a dead end. All she was left with was the thoughts of how good she must be at IT. Even still obviously none of those things were IT because IT would have made a way out of the shadows of her mind and reveal what IT was so that she could embrace IT and nurture IT. She wanted to be able to tell everyone that said they saw IT that she finally found IT. Another part of what she found was that some people will see IT and recognize IT yet do not want others to see IT especially since she hadn't found IT yet. Then there were others that saw IT and did not know what to do with IT so they didn't want to be bothered with IT because if she came to realize what IT was then they would have to explain what they have been doing with IT that was given to them.

Nevertheless, her journey seemed endless she came to a point where she said, "Forget IT!" IT doesn't want me to find IT she was just tired of looking for IT. She could not help but think "Well IT must not be all that if I can't find IT and no one wants to tell me what IT is."

Suddenly something hit her. She didn't know what IT was, but she began writing out a list of possible goals. As she was doing that she slowly came to see how after doing and trying so many things that the answer was right there, and she was the only one that couldn't see IT.

Now IT all seems clear she had to stop chasing IT and face her own fears.

Ridiculous

You can fit in everywhere and belong nowhere.
all that matters is
you are comfortable with yourself everywhere.
all the frustrations
from society's constant dictation and moral manipulation
the need to keep up with someone else
actually says that there is something missing within yourself
yet some sit in discontent
when someone else shows enough confidence
to not always follow the nonsense
those that understand their mentality
is part of their individuality
demonstrating what followers love to hate
understanding that everything the majority likes
isn't so great
we all like material things
and the temporary joy some of it brings
the problem is some get attached to so many of the wrong things
looking for status many times being reckless,
just to make someone's infamous checklist
there are times when I am rendered speechless
because some people can be so ridiculous
When you stop trying to fit in
you discover you shine from within

Ladies Night

From the suburbs to the hood
the power of sisterhood is all good
sometimes the ladies have to break out the stilettos
to let everything go
tonight, is not about any man
let every woman get a drink in her hand
toast the woman next to you
because with all our daily responsibilities
another woman is the only one who will understand you
just for a little while we get to let our hair down
with a ladies night on the town
inebriated bound a sense of freedom found
with no man or kids around
talking about everything between life and work,
flirting with jerks, devious smirks whatever works
a chance to let down our hair
and party without a care but when we're done
we leave all that stuff there
then once again back to the daily wearing of many hats
and the daily grind
but in the back of our minds
we think about those good times
we had with sisters of all kinds
wishing we didn't have to leave it all behind
but for a few hours
we stood together like a beautiful garden of flowers

walking in tennis shoes or stilettos and letting our cares go
and talking about things that only another woman knows
a reminder to take some time and clear your mind
treat yourself good
and enjoy at least one night of sisterhood
whether in the suburbs or the hood.

Unconditional Love

If I could change the world today
I would breathe life into angels that have passed away
giving them all a safe place to stay
I'd clone my heart a billion times
break them all into pieces and pass them out in lines
so everyone could feel loved all the time
everyone would eat no human being would skip a beat
the thirst for power and greed would be gone
and we would all basically get along
there would be minor problems
but always with a mutually peaceful way to solve them
division would fall, our race would say ALL
religion would be love
and nature will be able to just do what it does
simply because it was done out of peace
and unconditional love
everyone will still be unique beautiful inside
regardless of looks or physique,
acceptance of others would be a way of life
in the dictionary there's no definition or words
for hate or strife
AWW...what a pleasant getaway to see the world

Unfollow the Leader

She tried to play follow the leader
although she was never a believer
walking a fine line with no room in between
to pick a side to walk on made her scream
there were things on each side that would try to kill
a part of her whole being
making her question what's the meaning
constantly walking on a wire too thin for most
there were times when she tipped over and other times
where she just seemed to coast
but the tight rope walking act was getting old
from what she could tell
she knew the safety net was worn out
from catching her whenever she fell
but without it she would just descend into her own living hell
to get across she had to find another way
it can't be one way or the other as they say
if she stopped to evaluate her options
she would also have to maintain her balance
on a tight rope this is quite the challenge
knowing she couldn't stop moving
she decided she would create another way
so she just stepped off the wire one day
immediately she started falling
and fell right through a hole in the safety net right below
now in a state of panic wondering how long

and how far would this go
finally landing on a platform that was bigger
than the wire she was walking on
but she thought this must be wrong
no one mentioned that there was a platform
underneath all the trials and tribulations
she walked on the wire for so long
the leader never said there was more to it than it seemed
all she could see
was herself falling into a perpetual deep abyss in her dreams
she knew within herself there had to be something else
inside the lines that lie in between she became a leader to stop following leaders of other things.

Changing the Table

The idea of greatness is determined by what someone or something has continuously done, to go above and beyond living purposely in harmony to reach an elevated state. Yet the way human beings determine greatness is by who is deemed superior by reaching a certain level of achievement. Many claim that America is the greatest country ever established because of its many successes. While others will say that it's not so great nor has it ever been because of how these successes were achieved. The idea of the greatness of this country like beauty is in the eye of the beholder. It is with that in mind that we can debate the sentiment of making America great again and what that means to different people.

America the beautiful, land of the brave, the melting pot. These things we all have been fed as true. The one thing that has not been true for everyone is that America is or ever was great for everyone. To say that we must make America great again would imply that it was once a great country for everyone during some period of time. Yet since its proclaimed inception America has failed to reach a measurable amount of greatness for all its inhabitants. The standards and principles set forth in American society stem from the original immigrants religious and philosophical beliefs brought from their home countries. Therefore, it stands to reason that they would want to continue to control the way those beliefs are viewed and demonstrated as time passes. They are known as the controlling group. So logically the controlling group would also attempt to control who benefits from any laws and regulations set forth, that would set the guidelines for an overall success and be viewed as a contribution to this growing nation. As this is the case, all other groups are forced to meet the standards set forth by the controlling group, who has been willing and able to change the rules at any time to ensure their group reaps the benefits at the expense of everyone outside of that controlling group.

The first line from The U.S. Constitution "We the People" was written over two hundred years ago. The statement "We the People" originally only referred to the immigrants that invaded and stole the country from the indigenous people of the land. The writers of this document were not referring to people that did not look like them or originate from across the waters from which they came. This is what makes them the controlling group. I would say that wasn't a great start to a great country, as would those that were slaughtered and enslaved during the process. The writers of the Constitution took some of their core ideas from infamous philosophers such as John Locke, Charles de Secondat, Baron de Montesquieu, Jean-Jacques Rousseau and Thomas Hobbs who believed that people have inalienable rights. Inalienable rights are rights that cannot be taken away, denied, or transferred. Yet history has proven that these inalienable rights have only been applied to certain members of American society. That seemed to be a great time in America for those it benefitted but, what about everyone else?

The way American history is told to the masses, is as if this nation was founded on loving and humble principles that were to be applied to all human beings. If this were true, then there would have been no need to add amendments to this document that we hold to be the law of the land that we call The U.S. Constitution. It could be said that the added amendments were in an effort to achieve greatness. It seems the founding fathers were wise enough to know that things would have to change as the country grew, so they allowed for adjustments to be made to the document as the needs of the country would change. Often there is a failure to mention that every amendment added was specifically worded to protect the benefits of the descendants of those that were the original immigrants to this land. At the same time the added amendments only give crumbs off the table to those other than the controlling group. While all those considered to be "others", constantly pointed out they are supposed to be sitting at the table with them not just getting crumbs off the table when it is allowed. The problem is that the original immigrants stole the table and everything that came with it by way of force, violence, murder, and enslavement of the very people that offered them a seat at the table to begin with. Those are not humble and loving beginnings and was not a great time for any person not of European descent whose inalienable rights were not protected or respected. I guess for some that would be considered a great time in America because that's when America was established with the documents created by the original immigrants to back it up.

I suppose another period when America may have been viewed as great by some, was during the industrial revolution. This was a time when America started to make advancements that impacted not only America but the rest of the world giving it a stronger economic footing. Then again, it wasn't so great for those that were not allowed to capitalize on those times. Those seen as "others" were still not afforded the same liberties as the focus group of the founding fathers. These "other" groups included but were not limited to: Women, Black people, Indigenous people, and poor people to name a few. Yet all these groups and others were used to advance American society through various ways with little or no credit given to them. Some of the ways this has been done was through the theft of scientific discoveries, stolen technological advancements and the use of forced labor with little or no pay. If a person was not in the image of the founding fathers, then they were not allowed the same education, jobs, opportunities, lifestyle or respect. Many would argue that part of what makes America great, is the fact that you can come here from another country and make a life for yourself in the land of opportunity. Meanwhile they negate the fact that many have been denied opportunities because they belong to groups other than the controlling majority. Yes, it was a great time in America for the descendants of the original immigrants. Many of them were able to become pioneers and captains of industry leaving an American legacy. It did not seem to matter that their successes were achieved at the expense of and on the backs of all other groups that also inhabited America but were denied opportunities and their rights making it not so great for them. Leading to the questions what time in America are they referring to, and make it great again for who?

Apparently, in the eyes of the controlling group America is and always has been a great country. That was until America elected it's first black President in 2008. Since then, there has been unprecedented disrespect shown to the person holding the highest position in America. Any and everything he attempted to propose, or change was met with unscrupulous criticism and thwarted at every turn. After eight years of doing everything possible to ensure this President had no success in office, the controlling group then chose to spread the rhetoric that he hadn't done anything during his time in office to improve the country. Conveniently leaving out the fact they put roadblocks up at every turn. This was followed up with the notion that America needs to be made great again. Up until 2008 every single President of The United States had been in the image of the founding fathers, who were white males. None of the previous Presidents could create a level playing field for all the other groups that have been left out of the American dream. So, what could have changed that suddenly America was not a great country in their eyes? There had been 43 previous Presidents that have all left an impact on this country with their laws and policies whether good or bad. Each one was left with the mess the previous President created yet the greatness of America has never been questioned by the controlling group who shouted from the rooftops how great America was. The only thing that changed was the shift in the attitudes of the "other" groups. Seeing the first black President gave the "other groups" hope that this was a sign that there would be a shift in the culture of America, and its treatment of people that are not in the image of the previous 43 presidents or the original immigrants. Even with that hope the "other" groups still find the notion that America was great and needs to be made great again debatable.

It seems that for some people the only time America is great is when the people in power resemble the founding fathers. This ensures that their values and beliefs are demonstrated in the way they feel best suits members and descendants of the controlling group. It also ensures that they remain in control of all "other" groups and determine who benefits overall. To make America great again in the eyes of all the "other" groups, would mean to take away the hope that they would eventually be offered a seat at the table that had been denied since the inception of America. Making America great again would mean that there is a need to keep a level of superiority in favor of the original immigrants to America. Once again saying that only Christian, heterosexual, white males will be sitting at the table that was originally stolen, while choosing when to give others crumbs off the table. America the land of the brave where only a few are free, in a beautiful land that was supposed to be for you and me. America has only been great for the controlling group while all other groups will say that America was not so great in the first place. To make America great again surely depends on your point of reference.

Diverse Opinions on Diversity

The push for diversity in business affects every aspect of business across the globe. There are laws against discrimination in American society as it stands. Now there is the need to push for diversity in all aspects of business. Causing some companies to question whether they are diverse enough in their business practices. Diversity is defined as the condition of having or being composed of differing elements, variety; especially the inclusion of different types of people (as people of different races or cultures) in a group or organization. Discrimination is defined as the practice of unfairly treating a person or group of people differently from other people or groups of people or the ability to understand that one thing is different from another thing. Diversity and Discrimination are not the same thing but cover some of the same issues. The issue of diversity deals more with the conflicts that arises from the combining of different people of varying cultural backgrounds and how they can work together with respect for each other in an effort to accomplish a common goal.

The issues of a business being diverse enough comes into questions when there seems to be a conflict that manifests due to some cultural differences and misunderstandings. So, who decides whether a company is diverse enough and how do they determine if there are questions of diversity or discrimination seeing as the two are so closely related. There definitely is a need for safeguards in place because we know issues exist just to what extent and by whose definition.

To have safeguards for a business in place that shows they are diverse in practices and not practicing discrimination at the same time is needed for some of the reasons stated by JoAnne Miller Director of the Center for The New American Workforce. She says, "yes diversity policies for American businesses are good for American workers". She states, "that because different people from different parts of an organization are put together to solve problems it introduces new aspects of diversity to be managed". The reasons she gives seem to represent the idea of businesses interacting with every type of cultural aspect within a company or may encounter during the course of handling the needs of the business they represent. The goal of the employer is to be all inclusive as America itself is. Therefore, diversity policies are definitely needed when it comes to businesses doing business. Diversity surely increases business, but can it really be defined by one entity.

Everyone does not share the same views as it pertains to diversity because of discrimination laws already in place. For example, Frederick R. Lynch Associate Professor of Government at Claremont McKenna College says "the diversity policies are not needed when it comes to business". He states "that diversity policies are a political agenda rooted in three assumptions culled from – multiculturalism, numbers oriented affirmative action and the notion that generally everyone should be represented in every aspect of all American businesses". His stance is that the forcing of diversity policies in business will cause more tensions and lead to the over scrutinizing of words and behavior in the business world along with many of the policies that are already covered through discrimination laws in some form. Seeing as our population is so diverse it is almost impossible to cater to the needs and sensitivities of a culture and business along with attempting to balance personalities in the workplace for a common goal. The position he takes is understandable because in some ways a business would focus more on being sensitive to everyone's needs instead of taking care of the business.

Yes, we need diversity. Ms. Miller states that "the need for diversity policies mirror the changing demography within the world today that affects the very people that are employed by and run these businesses that interact with each other globally". Ms. Miller also stated that "Diversity has important implications for doing business: competencies that are required to be competitive in global markets, necessary knowledge, barriers to developing and coordinating talent, new ways of working and the development of business trust among diverse people". Mr. Lynch stated that "Diversity management theory and practice vary as widely as the policies' intended and unintended consequences. Politically neutral, cross-cultural training to improve sales and service for increasingly heterogeneous urban or international customer bases is probably useful". And employees welcome greater workplace flexibility through telecommuting, flextime and attentiveness to work-family issues. Both are stating that there are benefits for all involved in having diversity in business.

The issues of diversity are extremely complicated and not easily defined. It is not surprising that these two individuals have varying viewpoints on the issue regarding the need for diversity policies. Men are from Mars and Women are from Venus as they say. Their lifestyles are different starting with gender giving them opposing experiences at times that the other would not have experienced and that is only from the gender standpoint and not inclusive of other possible varying information that may include but not limited to race, class, education, sex, religion, and other ways we commonly use to classify people. Mr. Lynch falls into the majority category in various ways by default if he is a white-, religious-, middle- or upper-class heterosexual male which is and always has been the ruling majority in American society. The articles make no mention of any of these things except the fact he is male. Ms. Miller is in fact a female that is by default part of the minority which in part means that she has been disenfranchised at some point in her life not to mention if she herself does not fit into the classifying categories as Mr. Lynch in American society. Ms. Miller has never been a member of the majority even before we get to her race, class, education, sex etc. These different experiences as individuals living as male and female can classify as being diverse. Therefore, they will define diversity differently through no fault of their own and implement it differently based on their experiences.

Diversity seems to be based on who is not represented and how they are possibly being excluded based on the judgment of another party. As human beings we can be empathetic to the plight of the disenfranchised and agree that there should be a level playing field for all. Both Miller and Lynch agree that ensuring that businesses are inclusive of all cultures and demographics would raise their stakes in a global market but that is where the agreements end. While Ms. Miller maintains the need for not only discrimination laws but a need for diversity policies as well that will incorporate more of the multicultural aspects and demography of the American people in business globally that also reflects American culture, she also believes that there is a need to mandate those policies to address the changing demography at the same time and the issues they face along the way that are imperative to how they interact with other cultures. Mr. Lynch maintains that the current discrimination laws should serve as enough and that the diversity policies just pick apart and over analyze the discrimination laws already in place. He says instead re-emphasize the values of nondiscrimination and equal treatment does not create more policy that does more harm than good. Yet they both agree that there needs to be laws and/or policies in place to ensure that everyone gets a fair deal. They are both aware of the inequality in America which includes the workplace. They are indeed diverse in how they view the diversity issues that American businesses face.

One chooses to implement the broad stroke affect which in their eyes covers the smaller issues under one umbrella while the other chooses to implement the addressing of each facet of the broader strokes as some are not clearly covered under the umbrella. One thing they can agree on for sure is making sure American businesses in some way cater to the global market they just vary on the method of doing it. Which brings one to question how and who determines and/or defines that a business is diverse enough. Until we stop classifying people in various forms there will always need to be safeguards in place to protect people from forms of discrimination but do we need to dissect every aspect of conflicts that arise and claim cultural diversity?

That seems to be an ongoing question that is not going to be solved any time soon.

Suppose I Oppose

They try to tell me how someone like me is supposed to look
there are thousands of experts with thousands of books
but how can they tell me how to display my own reality
my performance isn't for them
it's just for me as I take away your power of agency
I emphatically oppose the views they impose on me
they look through rose colored lenses
oblivious of similar differences
their lenses aren't tinted their tainted
yet they expect me to accept the picture of me they have painted
when what they present visually is nothing like me
it is just a small representation
or aspect of a culture they observed momentarily

Let's see the standards that have been set for me
and others that live a different reality
we must meet the standards
that are based on European male views of beauty
while smiling, being nice, dainty, and clean,
always respectful while never saying anything we mean
along with fulfilling all the duties of mother, sister, and wife
sprinkled with princess and fairy dreams

Oh, isn't it a wonderful life
all while looking flawless and batting our eyelashes
because we know who the boss is

stilettos, fitting clothes, skirts and dresses
making sure that at least a little skin shows
if you don't believe me
look at the images displayed on the big and small screens
commercials, advertisements, and anything that is visually seen
google feminine beauty images and you will see what I mean

They have been setting the standards through their eyes
imposing their views of how they see others' lives
constantly reinforcing those views
to others looking through tainted lenses
leaving us who are labeled "other" to our own defenses
while still offending some of our senses
yet to some it does not make sense yet
visual perception can be truthful or pure deception
they conceptualize the performance displayed
with no consideration for the culture from which it came
all they see is that it's exotic and different
from what they have known to be the same

Therefore, I oppose the gaze that you have imposed on me
I will not surrender my power of agency
as I stated before the performance, I display is just for me
telling them to get their tainted rose-colored lenses cleaned
I'm with Bell Hooks using the oppositional gaze
when viewing what they say they have seen
mostly because the standards in place do not reflect others' reality
it was men who set the stage for how women should act and look
they are the ruling majority that's
so they control what's seen even in a book
I am opposed to the scenes that I have seen
supposedly representing my reality
they act like they don't know what I mean

because I'm part of the others'
redefining the line drawn in the sand and everything in between.

Vulnerable

She never had the luxury of vulnerability as it seemed others were blinded by the strength that was ingrained in her biology. Over time she had to work overtime to build a skin so thick that after awhile nothing penetrated it. Yet others were oblivious to what she endured to become like this. Heart closed with open eyes she stopped extending herself to others as there were too many times people tried to hide the sunrise. Determined not to be forever in the dark she decided to lay a new path where she could follow her heart in hopes to find the vulnerability she never lost but was forced to abandon at all costs.

Look

I went searching for dreams
that were not painted with beautiful nature scenes
I had to go in between the lines in search of a few things
Puppets don't dance on their own
they have choreographed moves,
in bewilderment they perform so dependent on the strings
they become afraid to see how they might dance on their own.

Unload

Somehow I'm supposed to be alright with all the apologies I never got. I'm supposed to suck it up and be the bigger person because the other person never gave another thought to the trauma they caused. They wanted to stop my free spirit because of the kind of spirit they think they got

Somehow it was okay for them to get on with their lives and leave me with unwanted gifts of mistrust, uncertainty, unresolved issues and boxes of invisible tissues. Nobody cares to se scars from broken hearts so we start walking around always on guard protected all our collected unhealed scars

Somehow it was alright to leave me hanging by a thin thread as you ran to safety right before you cut the thread, I was leaving it for you to come across to safety. Somehow, I'm supposed to accept you emotional ignorance in silence. I'm supposed to take the venom you spit as well as swallow it. I'm supposed to accept that you tried to take me out with precision.
Then again
I can't be you. I love until love no longer comes through. I love because it allows me to choose to see the love in you. I love because it feels good too. What trauma happened to you that you won't allow someone to love or show love to you. Somehow, someway something has sucked, kicked or killed the love right out of you. So now you're scared to let any love come shining through to bounce off of or rub off on anyone around you

Somehow, we all realize in some way we didn't get a fair deal. Coming to terms with our own form of trauma so we can face it and learn how to deal. At some point we have to start loving ourselves enough to unload all the baggage and trauma bestowed upon us by others so we can build ourselves up. That is the only way we will ever start to level the playing field. Unload one thing at a time then step back and watch what it will reveal. Unload so you can give them back all the unwanted gifts they gave in an unfair deal.

Fragile

In movies they always have that main female character that is viewed as the epitome of fragility at the beginning of the film and as it progresses you see the evolution of that female character and how she got that way. She goes from being extremely delicate and fragile to being a pillar of strength. It's not easy for her to get there depending on the plot of the story but she always manages to get there by the end of the movie. At the end everyone stands and cheers for the resilient woman who overcame everything that was put in her way to destroy her and yet we thought she was so fragile.

Problem with that scenario is that most times the fragile women that fight the hardest fights never seem to reflect the visual you see in the movies. There is this presumption that fragile is to look a certain way on women. Each person has their own ideals and/or perceptions of what fragile women look like whether they admit it out loud or not. Whatever the visual that you assign to being fragile it will in some way mirror what is given as a visual in film. This means there are millions of women around the world in a fragile state at any given time that are overlooked because they do not look the part according to what the world has been told a fragile woman looks like.

The people that an overlooked fragile woman would assist would be the same ones that think she doesn't require assistance while forming their lips to say catchphrases like "God gives some of his toughest soldiers the toughest battles" or the let me absolve myself of offering any assistance by simply saying "I'll pray for you" accompanied by a Cheshire Cat grin. Although some will watch from a distance to see if you've made any progress with your issue. Then they can come back and say "Look at God I was praying for you". Then there are times when you rather some people didn't help as their help comes with a price they would never charge someone they viewed as fragile. Half the time they don't even think she's in a fragile state because she doesn't carry the weight of the world the same as they do in the movies about evolving fragile women so they assume she can afford the price of their assistance.

The difference is when a woman that learned to overcome her hardships, obstacles and learned to maneuver in a fragile state while still helping others and not receiving the same amount of assistance to repair her own fragile state in return is almost always viewed as overly confident, incapable of vulnerability, aggressive and a plethora of other adjectives that would never be ascribed to a "typical fragile woman" that has been deemed resilient and kept moving forward. Of course when considered resilient no one thought she was fragile because she looked like she didn't need help so no one asked although she asked because she had been through a lot that made her temporarily fragile.

Go figure.

Irreplaceable

To make it in this world they said I would have to put on a face
that I simply could not create,
so I decided to create my own place in the world
where I never have to put on a face
as the original me cannot be replaced.

The Contortionist

She had different looks that all looked the same
her only claim to fame was being a body trying to get in the game
while her mouth spewed venom to hide her pain

Serendipity

That one time I lost my mind
I found it sitting and contemplating
with other things I forgot I left behind.

A Moment

Numbing the feeling to delay a reaction
just to insure you don't give pain and
disappointment any satisfaction
A tangled web of disbelief in order to avoid grief
that ultimately may only be brief.

Veronica Thornton known to most as "Vee" is from Cleveland, Ohio. Some of her previous works include but are not limited to several poetic anthologies published by Creative Talents Unleashed publishing, contributing writer for former online magazines Poets Unlimited and Eloquently Speaking. She also had the opportunity to have one of her poems "Unbeaten Path" included in the 2016 Ohio Poetry Association's journal "Common Threads" not to long after releasing her first full length book of poetry "Universal Colloquies Inside of Me". In less than a decade she is contributed to over 10 books of poetry 2 works of nonfiction along with a few journals and magazines.

Vee
Raw Glass
Photography

"I'm too close to beginning to even consider being close to finished."
Vee

What they Said

Veronica Thornton a.k.a. Vee follows up on her first book of poetry "Universal Colloquies Inside of Me" with this collection of writings that go beyond poetry. Vee has taken advantage of several opportunities to grow as a writer lending her pen to several books on varying subjects exhibiting her versatility in writing styles.

Here is what Readers have said:

"5.0 out of 5 stars This is a book for everyone to read!

"One of the most unique collections I've read. The topics vary from one end of the spectrum to the other when looking inside the human psyche. It has a large cross section of topics that reaches out to every mind set."
        T. Thompson

"If you're looking for intellectual poetry with a philosophical nature then look no further. This collection is incredibly thought provoking & inspiring. "
    L. Diego

Vee's Links

Facebook
www.facebook.com/PhilosophyinPoetry

Instagram
@Philosophyinpoetry

Website

www.veesphilosophyinpoetry.com

www.ingramcontent.com/pod-product-compliance
Lightning Source LLC
Chambersburg PA
CBHW031256290426
44109CB00012B/609